No Th
I'm 1662

Cartoons
at the Giving of the Peace

Jim Cotter
& Stuart Yerrell

CAIRNS PUBLICATIONS · SHEFFIELD
ARTHUR JAMES · BERKHAMSTED

This edition published in Great Britain in 1998 by

CAIRNS PUBLICATIONS
47 Firth Park Avenue, Sheffield S5 6HF

in association with

ARTHUR JAMES LTD
70 Cross Oak Road, Berkhamsted, Herts HP4 3HZ

[First published in 1988 by Cairns Publications]

A catalogue record for this book is available
from the British Library.

ISBN 0 85305 458 4

Typeset in Monotype Columbus by
Strathmore Publishing Services, London N7.

Printed in Great Britain by
Ipswich Book Company, Ipswich, Suffolk.

Contents

Preface   v

Preface to the second edition   vi

A Controversial Custom   1

Cartoons   13

Preface

I couldn't help smiling. Changes were afoot in the Church of England, and nobody quite knew what to expect next. My neighbour's response to my greeting. 'The Peace of Christ be with you,' was a surprised 'Thank you very much.' That was some years ago now, but as is the way of these things, the fund of stories has grown. Then a friend suggested making a collection and publishing them as a book of cartoons. So here it is.

It has been a delight to me that Stuart Yerrell, one of my oldest friends (not, I hasten to add, one of my most elderly friends), agreed to draw the cartoons. My memory had been stirred by the way in which he used to amuse us at school and chapel with his ingenuous funny drawings – and that was thirty or more years ago. So I am grateful to him for this modest gallery of recognizable characters.

My thanks also go to the people who sent me stories and captions, among them Elaine Adam, Helena Astley, Mary Beardshaw, Graham Blacktop, Austin Boggis, Helen Bridel, Alan Christmas, Kathleen Gardner, Martin Gardner, Roy Harrison, Olwen Holmes, Primrose Kite, Muriel Landon, Brian Macdonald-Milne, Judy Mann, S. McCullagh, John McNutt, Jo Rivers, Jessie Rothera, K. H. Rudolph, Sari Salvesen, Julie Sinclair, Ingrid Slaughter, P. Spivey, Eugene Suggett, Frank Walker, Duncan Wilkins. If I have omitted any name, my apologies, and due acknowledgment will be made in any future editions.

I hope this collection will provoke reflection as well as

amused recognition. It may be that laughter, whether wry, rueful, or jovial, is really what is next to godliness.

JIM COTTER
Exeter
August 1988

Preface to the second edition

This modest nudge of a book has been out of print for some years, and I am glad that my new association with Arthur James Ltd gives it a new lease of life. I have been asked for it regularly, and I have seen it referred to not only by parish magazines (that of Berkhamsted but a month or so ago), but also in the magazine of the Prayer Book Society. Their readers, a number of whom wrote for copies only to find none available, will be among the first to hear of this new edition!

The cartoons are unaltered, but there are a couple of additions to the Introduction, and a few amendments.

Oh yes, I nearly forgot. In the second paragraph of the original Preface, for 'thirty' substitute 'forty'...

JIM COTTER
Sheffield
January 1998

A Controversial Custom

Of bishops and parish clerks

I enjoyed the story of the bishop who had become restless during a long service in a cathedral. The preacher had spoken for half an hour and the intercessions had been of the extended kind that wearies the human ear if not the divine. At the Peace, the bishop is reputed to have responded to his chaplain, 'I need more than peace. If this were the Orthodox Church the bishop would be given sherry and cake at this point in the proceedings.'

I don't know if that story is true, though I rather hope it is. I am however assured by various correspondents that they have severally heard the 'captions' to the cartoons in this book. Clearly the Peace is a custom which vexes some and heartens others. I trust that the cartoons will offend neither.

The tone is lighthearted, but the response to this twentieth century revival of an ancient custom has not been wholehearted. Not that the Church of today is the first to find it a cause of strife: a correspondent from Essex sent me a quotation from the magazine of the parish of Theydon Garnon, which included an account of an incident in the sixteenth century. At that time it was the duty of the parish clerk to pass to each person in the congregation 'the Pax', which was a kind of ikon, a painting, probably on wood, of the Annunciation or Nativity or other scene from the life of Christ. In about 1520, the clerk was a certain Mr Pond. He had to take care to present the Pax strictly in order of social precedence, and on the Sunday before All Saints' Day he seems to have got it wrong. He went first to a Mrs Hampden and then to a Mr Brown who, 'instead of kissing it, grabbed it and cracked it down on Mr Pond's head ...' (There was some dispute afterwards as to exactly how many drops of blood had been drawn and whether the flow had in any way desecrated the church.)

Well, the Peace does not sit easily with hierarchical pride: Chaucer's Parson in *The Canterbury Tales* was aware that the chief of the deadly sins waited to ensnare the one who looked to kiss the Pax before his neighbour.

The embarrassed English

A stiff upper lip usually prevails, it seems, in modern England: accounts in 1997 of its being in terminal tremble may be premature. Even a handshake feels inappropriate to some, despite its origin in the assurance one man gave to another that he was not concealing a weapon. In one church a woman was particularly persistent in trying to greet a man who was doing his best to ignore her. 'I'm trying to give you the Peace,' she said. His response was a dry, 'We're not at war, are we?' Some weeks later there was another attempt at 'conversation', this time at a parish gathering: 'Hello, we've met before.' 'Oh yes, you tried to do something to me in church.' Some will smile at that, others will nod ruefully in sympathy. What feels like a genuinely friendly gesture to some will be received by others as an intrusion, an attempt at enforced intimacy. One correspondent suggested to me that 'Goodbye' was appropriate, in its original sense of 'God be with you,' a wish he felt was 'pious, benevolent, and British'. And there is the story of the elderly woman who felt that one greeting was enough, and replied to a girl in the choir, 'No thanks, dear, I've already had it.' Or there is the man who said, 'Not this morning, Dave, I don't feel like it.' I am told that some members of one congregation took to holding up placards on which were written, 'I do not wish to shake hands.' That is rather like the 'peace-free zone' of the cover of this book, or the sign, 'No touch pews in north aisle.' One vicar is said to have muttered 'Kiss of Peace? My lot need the kiss of life.'

The impromptu informal message is also quite popular: 'Congratulations on passing your driving test.' 'Would you like a lift home?' 'He can't find his Mum.' More sardonic humour came from two responses thought up to 'No thank you, I'm 1662.' One was, 'You don't look that old;' another, 'Ah, I'm Charles II and you must be Nell Gwynne.' And there is a rumour that some people wished to revive the old custom of pew rents, reserving their own seat next to the aisle where they knew the handsome (or beautiful) new vicar would give the Peace to those so favourably positioned.

Mixed indeed are the motives of the human heart. And somehow a local church has to find ways of containing the extroverts who like boundless embraces, seeking to envelop every other member of the congregation in turn, and the more reserved who are thankful if the pillars are thick enough to hide behind (or slowly to circle around) during the fray. Even an episcopalian Californian was heard to mutter that he had had enough of 'hugfests'.

The custom has been criticized even in the House of Commons. Last year (1997) there was a debate on ecclesi-astical matters, these days always providing quotable eccen-tricities. Indeed, Simon Hoggart, reporting in the *Guardian*, felt that the antics of MPs had much in common with the more informal kinds of church services. 'In fact there can be quite a happy-clappy air in Parliament. The congregation cheers, applauds, and laughs dementedly for no apparent reason. Perfectly ordinary speeches are greeted by cries of 'Hosanna!' and 'Praise be' or their equivalent. All that is missing are the tambourines and electronic keyboards, and of course the bit where you get to snog the person next to you. That goes on outside the Chamber.' He then reports Mr Banks who sprang up to declare: 'People don't go to church to be felt up by the person next to them in the pew. They want the Hand of God laid on them, not the hand of some stranger.'

The playwright Alan Bennett has admitted in his diaries, *Writing Home*, that he dreads the moment of 'fellowship', but was humbled by the genuine kindness of the greeting given him by a regular member of the congregation at a funeral in his local Roman Catholic church.

If you are offering your gift ...
And that story might indicate that frivolity has its limits. Indeed one parish priest, appalled by what he perceived as superficial bonhomie, preached a scathing sermon in which he said that the custom would cease until the peace of Christ was a reality in the congregation. He reminded them of the Gospel saying, 'If you are offering your gift at the altar, and there remember that your brother has something against you, leave your gift there before the altar and go; first be reconciled to your brother, and then come and offer your gift.' (Matthew 5:23) It was this verse that probably first led the Church to place the Peace before the Offertory in the Eucharist, though by the fifth century its position in

the service at Rome had moved to a point just preceding
Communion, in which place it remains to this day. And the
verse is echoed in the bidding to Confession in the older
Anglican prayer books where the Peace itself is not
included, 'Ye that do truly and earnestly repent you of your
sins, and are in love and charity with your neighbours ...'

Here we have gone beyond the embarrassment, the un-
ease, and the class distinctions which are expressed, as such
discomfort often is, by humour. We are certainly confused.
What touch is appropriate in greeting others in our pluralistic culture and in mobile ecumenical days? Perhaps these
very human reactions were also a cause of the Peace being
omitted from the new prayer books in English at the time
of the Reformation, though the main reason was probably
a reaction against what was perceived as superstitious
idolatry in kissing the wooden Pax.

The Peace of Christ
However, the custom of the Peace, while not solemn, is
serious. Confession and absolution, the recognition of our
failure to love and the assurance of forgiveness, are condi-
tions of the peace of Christ becoming a reality. This is
difficult enough one-to-one in close human relationships,
let alone among a large body of people with their individual and corporate relationships with one another and with
God, many of whom, if we are honest, we do not particularly like (but whom, nevertheless, we may be called to
learn to love).

No wonder there is often a faint air of unreality about
the liturgical custom. Most of the time we live uneasily
between Jeremiah's despairing cry about the prophets and
priests of his day, 'They have healed the wound of my

people lightly, saying, 'Peace, peace,' where there is no peace,' (Jeremiah 6:14) and the yearning for the fulfilment of God's promise that Shalom will characterize the true and lasting reign of God, a community, a kingdom, a domain, a commonwealth, where men and women will live in right relationship with one another, in reconciliation and justice and mutual well-being and flourishing, a harmony shared by nature too. The story from Essex does at least indicate that the focus of the custom was right, however abused: it is the peace of *Christ* that should be our concern, its celebration and its anticipation.

Similarly, there is a tension often apparent these days at the communion itself. Some clergy use the first name of the communicant before the words 'The Body of Christ'. The concern to be humanly friendly rather than coldly formal is worthy, but the gesture can so easily take the focus away from the body of Christ that is being given, however much the human relationships may be 'in Christ'. And at the precise moment when we are all physically and verbally equal before God, the stranger next to me hears my name but not his own – a subtle distinction which makes the atmosphere actually less friendly than is intended.

Moreover, both these actions, the Communion and the Peace, are *rituals*, with a degree of formality implied which should neither unnecessarily disturb the reserved nor allow the enthusiastic free rein. It is a symbolic gesture, conveying at least a 'sample', a 'first fruits' of that which it symbolizes. At the deepest level, like all Christian ritual, its aim is to disturb us out of our complacencies and to be a sober reminder that enthusiasm is no reliable guide to the depth of commitment to the Peace and to the Body of Christ.

The Peace in the early years of the Church

The custom is impeccably ancient (not of course, in itself, a clinching argument for reviving or continuing it). But we cannot now know the complete range of meaning and experience behind the exhortations of St Paul and St Peter: 'Greet one another with a holy kiss,' (Romans 16:16) and 'Greet one another with the kiss of love. Peace be to all of you that are in Christ.' (1 Peter 5:14) Certainly this kind of greeting had been incorporated into the worship of at least Justin Martyr's church by the second century. In his Apology he wrote: 'At the conclusion of the prayers we greet one another with a kiss. Then bread and a chalice containing wine mixed with water are presented to the one presiding over the brethren.'

For Justin Martyr it seems as if the Peace was a way of sealing the prayers that preceded it, perhaps like an extended congregational Amen. But we do not know what individual reconciliations for what hurts had preceded the gathering for worship, nor do we know exactly what the sharing of the Peace would have meant to a company of Christians for whom the 'world' outside was often enough hostile, nor how eagerly a particular congregation would be yearning for the reign of Christ in all its glory. How did people of that time experience the actual physical touch of the Peace? Did they in practice experience the embarrassing border country between the affectionate and the overtly sexual, or is that a modern hazard? We may like to think that their faith and practice had a coherence that ours lacks and to which we may look back wistfully, but that is probably to oversimplify the past.

Anticipation of a fuller peace

Then as now I expect it was hard to speak the truth in
love, with the look of the eye and the touch of the hand
expressing intimacy without intrusion or possessiveness,
and truth without evasion or hypocrisy. Deeply to speak
the truth in love would indeed be to bring 'sacrament-
ally' alive, if only for a moment, something of what is
meant by the phrase 'the peace of Christ.' For the relationship of bodies in a body of people, however appro-
priately restrained, does symbolize, convey, express the
quality of that relationship. Do we in practice allow the
Spirit of Christ to shape our bodily relating so that we
know and show forth the reconciliation and harmony
(after all, it isn't just an idea) that would be a true anticipation of the Shalom of God for the whole universe?

In turning to greet a fellow member of the Body of
Christ, it is realistic for me to admit that I am not yet
totally at peace with *all* my neighbours. This might make
me hesitate so much that I become overscrupulous and
perfectionist and refuse to greet anybody this side of the
fulfilment of God's peace. But it would certainly be hypo-
critical of me to say the words 'The Peace of Christ' without a sincere intention of *seeking* that deeper and more
complete peace. (Indeed, I hope that I might be able to
greet my enemy in that way, even if not in church – and
at a wary distance.)

What gesture?

In a world and church where the boundaries of cultures and
forms of faith are confused, it is impossible for civil customs
to give a clue as to an appropriate gesture to accompany the
greeting of the Peace. In this country a handshake is

probably the easiest, but there are some who never touch
on greeting any but their closest family and friends, while
others are happy to peck cheeks or lightly (or heavily)
embrace. A handclasp might seem warmer to some, but
again embarrassingly effusive to others. I personally like the
custom of the Church of South India, in whose prayer book
is the rubric: 'The "Peace" may be given here. The giver
places his right palm against the right palm of the receiver,
and each closes his left hand over the other's right hand.' I
suspect that in India this is often accompanied by the slight
bow of the head which acknowledges the presence of God
in the other. I know that is not familiar to us in the West,
but the custom has a warmth *and* dignity, an intimacy *and* a
respect for and reverence of the other.

There is always the problem that a strange custom
(which actually means nearly all of Christian worship to
many people in our secularized society) tends to be exclu-
sive. And this is what we do not want a gesture of inclu-
siveness to be. I am aware that certain societies have
particular gestures (sometimes secret) to convey their common membership to one another. But how clear cut should
a Christian community be in demonstrating its boundaries,
and how much should a newcomer be expected to learn?
This is part of a much wider and deeper problem about the
impoverishment of symbols in a religion which may claim
to be universal in significance but which is not so in practice, at the same time as living in a pluralistic world. But
some would argue fiercely that we should do nothing at the
Eucharist that would unnecessarily exclude, that we should
have a policy of an 'open table' at communion, that anyone
drawn to participate should be free to do so. Would they
think the invitation genuine if they were caught up in a

custom so unfamiliar that they were bound to feel ex-
cluded? On the other hand, there is much detail in worship
that will feel strange to the newcomer, and the opportunity
of learning to relax into a gesture that is both predictable
and expressive, may enhance the quality of that individual's
worship as well as the corporate life of the whole
congregation.

In some churches, the Peace, with whatever expression,
is shared informally among those who happen to be sitting
near one another. In others it is passed in due hierarchical
order from the President to the assistant ministers, and
thence to the choir and congregation. Some of the demo-
cratically educated baulk at this, but it can be balanced
(some would say overturned) if at communion itself the
congregation receive first and the clergy last. Another
variant is for the President to give the Peace to two
children, who in turn help it to spread throughout the
church. (Perhaps the children themselves should be invited
to begin the action. They usually take rituals more seriously
and perform them more competently than the vast majority
of adults.)

The informal and the ritual

In order that the Peace may be experienced ritually yet
meaningfully, as the Peace of Christ, it might be helpful if
we placed elsewhere that human contact without which
congregations are accused of being unwelcoming and un-
friendly. (Then we would not be reproached by the last
cartoon in this book.) Those who criticize the Peace most
strongly seem to do so on the grounds that it distracts them
from the worship of God. If by this is meant, 'I am here to
worship God in my own individual way and other people

can be a distraction,' I think such grounds must be questioned. The prayer of the individual in church of course has its place, but Christian worship is a *corporate* activity of a *body* of people. However, the criticism has point if it refers to the way in which worship can appear to be little more than a cosy or noisy gathering of those who enjoy one another's company, a kind of ecclesiastical bingo with creche provided. While the shy and retiring might need help to appreciate the presence of children at the Eucharist, we all need help in becoming more sensitive to the way in which we try to worship the holy and mysterious and loving God. Might our critic's point be met if before the service began, strangers were acknowledged and welcomed and greetings exchanged (perhaps informally among the congregation in churches which often have visitors). Such introductions, which could include information about anything unusual in the service, could end more formally with 'The Lord be with you ... And also with you.'

Incidentally, to avoid the infelicitous 'And also with you,' could we not try something like this:

The God of Love be with you,

followed by the response,

The Holy Spirit dwell within you.

Or this:

We meet in the fellowship of the Holy Spirit.

May the grace of the Lord Jesus be with you,

followed by the response,

May the Love of God dwell in your heart.

These greetings could lead into a period of silence, out of which could be prayed the Collect for Purity (which begins, 'Almighty God, to whom all hearts are open ...'), in turn followed by the Invitation to Confession, Confession,

Kyries, Absolution, Peace, Gloria. This is not quite the usual order, but may be pastorally more helpful. In any case, does not some such beginning ease us into worship from first acknowledging who and where we are and acknowledging the presence of others around us? If there were an effective silence at the beginning of worship we would not need to feel embarrassed by a certain amount of informality beforehand.

At the end of the service could come the more established coffee and conversation, with a pastoral awareness, in a spirit of courteous friendship, of those who are visitors or newcomers, and of the lonely, the not so bright, and the not so glossy.

A further incidental though related point is that the information-giving of the Notices could be translated into biddings for prayer and so serve as a way in to the Intercessions, leaving the occasional announcement to the beginning of the service or to the informal gathering afterwards.

Then the Giving of the Peace could take its proper ritual place without interrupting the flow of the worship. The whole ethos of the Eucharist might then demonstrate this Peace of Christ on which we have focused for a moment or two at the Pax itself. Our difficulties in handling conflict creatively in church and society without harming or destroying one another require at least a faint echo in our worship.

Cartoons

at the Giving of the Peace

No thank you, I'm 1662.

I don't agree with it.

The Peace may be given in parishes of the
diocese so long as nobody touches.

Why, thank you ma'am, I sure do
appreciate that.

Mr Pond, Parish Clerk, Theydon Garnon,
c. 1520.

And the same to you, chum.

Peace to you – and get your dogs off my dog.

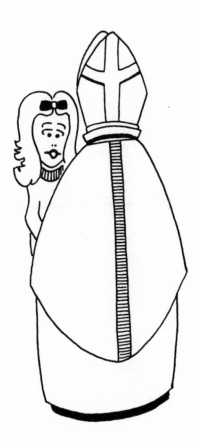

Ooo! Your hands *are* cold.

Good morning!

I don't need it – give it to someone who does.

Peace be with you –
and congratulations on the driving test.

Goodbye!

Pax vobiscum, mate.

Piece of what?

Thank you very much.

Oh, are you going now! Goodbye.

****** off!

And the same to you.

Wilkommen!

**** off.

– Peace be with you.
– Eh?
– The Peace of the Lord be with you.
– What's that supposed to mean?
– Oh, forget it.

Cheers, old man.

Zere is ze good Eenglish beeshop veez all zose
veemen saying, 'Peess, peess'.

Is it time to go home?

How do you do, bishop?

My dear man, we haven't been introduced.

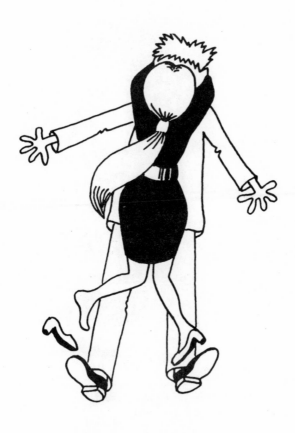

[Love at first sight.]

Thank you. This is the only time in the week
when someone touches me.